Andy Pandy

and

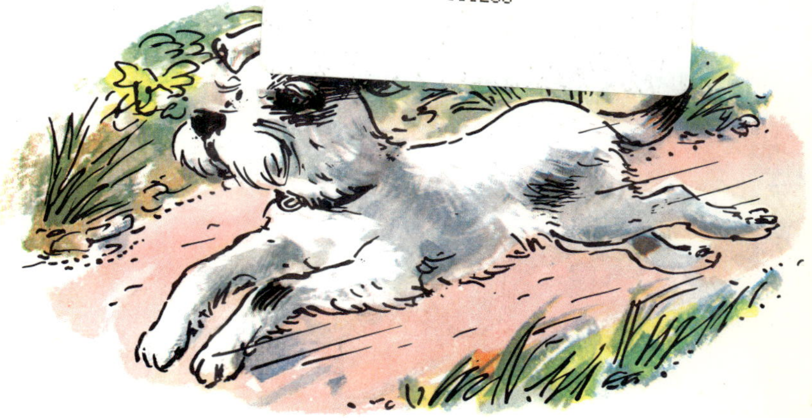

Story by Maria Bird

Illustrated by Matvyn Wright

HODDER AND STOUGHTON

LONDON SYDNEY AUCKLAND TORONTO

Andy Pandy's White Kitten likes eating, but he isn't a greedy little cat, so when one day he cried to be fed a few minutes after he had had his breakfast, Andy said, 'You can't be hungry already.' He went to the back door to look at the kitten's saucer.

There the kitten's saucer stood and it was quite empty. 'Are you really hungry?' he said as he picked the saucer up. 'Meeow,' cried the White Kitten standing on his hind legs with his front paws on Andy's rompers.

As soon as Andy had put more food in the saucer, the kitten fell upon it as if he had never had anything to eat. Teddy watched him, then he said, 'He was terribly hungry. *I* think Rags must have eaten his breakfast.'

Just then Rags came running up. As soon as he came near to the White Kitten, Teddy cried, ‘Go away, bad dog, you stole the White Kitten’s breakfast.’ Rags just looked at Teddy. He didn’t even bark.

Then he turned away and ran down the garden path. 'He's sorry, I expect,' said Andy. 'He'll come back soon.' But he didn't even when it was dinner-time. Andy filled the kitten's saucer again, and then went into the garden to fetch him.

But when he came back with the kitten in his arms, the saucer was empty again. ‘Teddy,’ he cried, ‘the kitten’s food has gone, so Rags must be somewhere in the garden. Let’s go and look.’ He put down some milk for the kitten.

Teddy was playing with Looby Loo. He put her on the window-sill and said, 'You watch for naughty Rags.' Of course he was only pretending, but as soon as Andy and Teddy went out, Looby jumped up and looked out of the window.

And what did she see?
A GREAT BIG
YELLOW DOG.
The White Kitten ran away
as soon as he saw him, and
with one lick of his tongue
he finished the milk and
sent the saucer flying.

Looby Loo banged on the window just as Andy and Teddy were coming back. They hadn't found Rags, but they did see the great big yellow dog jump over the hedge and run away.

'Teddy,' cried Andy Pandy, 'it wasn't Rags at all, so now we must go and find him.' Teddy began to cry, because it was he who had sent him away. The White Kitten cried too, and all three were in tears as they set off.

But Looby Loo thought she knew where Rags would be, and as soon as the others were out of sight, she jumped off the window-sill and ran out into the wood.

And there, at the foot of a big tree, she found him, looking very miserable. She told him all about the great big yellow dog, and how sorry Teddy was, and that they had all gone to look for him. 'Come along now,' she said.

But Rags wouldn't. 'Teddy thought I'd done it,' he said. 'He knows I would never touch the White Kitten's breakfast. He sent me away.' He had real tears in his eyes. 'Oh dear,' said Looby, 'now they're all crying.'

Suddenly Rags stopped crying and pricked up his ears. ‘Someone’s coming,’ he said. ‘Rags,’ cried Looby Loo, ‘it’s Andy Pandy and Teddy. They mustn’t find me here. Quick, let’s go home.’ ‘Jump on my back,’ said Rags.

In a second they were off, and as soon as they were back Looby climbed up on to the window-sill, and Rags ran off to find Andy and Teddy. Everybody hugged everybody, and they never saw the great big yellow dog again.

ANDY PANDY BOOKS

Andy Pandy and the Green Puppy
Andy Pandy and the Badger
Andy Pandy and the Patchwork Cat
Andy Pandy's Little Goat
Andy Pandy and the Scarecrow
Andy Pandy's Dovecot
Andy Pandy and the Teddy Dog
Andy Pandy's Washing Day
Andy Pandy and the Hedgehog
Andy Pandy Paints His House
Andy Pandy and the White Kitten
Andy Pandy's Jack-in-the-box
Andy Pandy's New Pet
Andy Pandy in the Country
Andy Pandy's Weather House
Andy Pandy's Shop
Andy Pandy's Red Motor Car
Andy Pandy and the Willow Tree
Andy Pandy and the Gingerbread Man
Andy Pandy and the Snowman
Andy Pandy's Playhouse
Andy Pandy and the Spotted Cow
Andy Pandy and the Yellow Dog
Andy Pandy's Puppy
Andy Pandy's Baby Pigs